BLOGGING FOR JESUS

Why You Should Start a Christian Blog and How to Do It

Donald L. Hughes

Theatron Books, San Diego, California

Donald L. Hughes

Blogging for Jesus

Why You Should Start a Christian Blog and How to Do It

Copyright © 2017-2018 by Donald L. Hughes. All Rights Reserved.

Published by Theatron Books - San Diego, California

See Legal Notices, Disclaimers and Credits at the end of this book.

ISBN: 978-1521442081

Donald L. Hughes is Editor of ChristianWritingToday.com
View hundreds of articles for Christian writers.

If you gain benefit from this book,
please leave a review at Amazon.com. **Thank you.**

What You'll Discover in this Book

Want to change the world with the message of Christ? Better hurry, because a cloud of evil is bringing darkness to it faster than ever before. The clock is approaching midnight, so now is the time to rescue the perishing. This book will explain one effective way to do that.

This book is different any other on this topic. Sure, it give you all the nuts and bolts about how to set up a blog, how to write blog posts and all the rest. I even tell you how you can receive an income from your blogging ministry. But more than that, I give you a *strategy* for reaching people. That is what sets this book apart.

What strategy do I suggest? Well, there is little point in setting up a teaching or preaching blog at this point in the decay of the world. There are already hundreds of thousands of those and if they worked, the world would not be in its present condition. You can add another one of those to the blogosphere if you wish, but so many people are twisting the truth of the Bible in so many ways that it's unlikely that you'll get a readership.

What strategy will you discover in this book? It's "relationship blogging." That's where you connect with people based on shared interest (something you know about and is of interest to others) and then lead them gently into a saving knowledge of Jesus Christ. Your blog may be about building hot rods, growing roses, or one of a thousand other topics, but no matter what — you're blogging for Jesus.

Is this a radical new approach? No, it's precisely the method that Jesus used when he engaged the woman at the well in John 4. I explain exactly how you can do that in the blogosphere in this book.

Donald L. Hughes

CONTENTS

CONTENTS 2

: 1 : Jesus Blogger 4

: 2 : A Blogging Strategy for the 21st Century 10

: 3 : Blogging Basics 17

: 4 : How to Select Your Topic 23

: 5 : An Overview of the Writing Process 29

: 6 : How to Construct a Blog Post 34

: 7 : Scheduling Posts 40

: 8 : How to Build a Readership 47

: 9 : Income Options 55

: 10 : How to Set Up Your Blog 61

: 11 : Use Your Blog as a Launch Platform 71

: 12 : A Blessing on Christian Bloggers 79

A Biblical Basis for Christian Relationship Blogging 83

About the Author 88

End Notes 89

Legal Notices and Disclaimers 91

Donald L. Hughes

:1:
JESUS BLOGGER

A Christian friend of mine has a blog. He hasn't been happy with the direction it's been going recently, so he asked me what he should do about it.

I had plenty of "nuts and bolts" ideas about his writing, how he was doing Search Engine Optimization (SEO), the visual look of his site and a few other things.

However, he wasn't asking about that. He was asking a deeper question. He was ruminating about whether blogging was a good use of his time. That's an important question. Our time on earth is a precious commodity and we always want to use it effectively.

I could only share from my own experience and tell him to keep on blogging for Jesus. Why did I offer that advice to him, and now to you? Here are the reasons.

REACH THE WORLD FROM YOUR LAPTOP

The Lord has given me many opportunities to travel and share the Gospel around the world from the South Seas to Siberia.

I've been able to share the Good News in places as diverse as a tiny church in Wikiup, Arizona and prisons that were once part of the old Soviet Gulag in Siberia. I have been chased by armed Ingush rebels in Russia and escaped angry Serbs at a UN Kosovo border crossing.

Besides preaching, I also shared the Gospel as an educator. But literature ministry has always been my main work— writing and editing books, magazine articles, newsletters and web posts in the hundreds—all to further the cause of Christ.

At a certain point, I could no longer travel. I started a Christian website and in a short time, I was reaching more than 50,000 people per month. I was reaching far more people around the world each month than I did in the previous decades of traveling.

I learned that I could reach the world from my laptop computer. That's why my focus is on how to use a blog to reach people for Christ, not just to engage other Christians. The kind of blog I talk about here is primarily an outreach tool.

The strategy is to create a blog on a topic that interests a wide range of people. It's not about the Bible or theology. It is tips for moms, how to take better pictures, how to make money online, nutrition—or one of ten thousand other topics. Draw people in with information that will enrich their lives. You infuse your blog, using tact and wisdom, with Christian values. You do not preach; you share your faith in a gentle and positive way and draw people to Christ.

There will always be a need for missionaries to travel the world to share the Gospel. However, a blog can be an effective way to reach huge numbers of people. In 1995 less than 1% of the population had Internet access. Ten years later, 1 million people were Internet users. Just five years after the number reached 2 billion. Just four years later (2014), the number reached 3 billion and it is rapidly approaching 4 billion people. That's about half the population of the world.[1]

I sold that website to a large ministry and focused my attention on ChristianWritingToday.com. My purpose is to train and inspire Christian writers, thus multiplying my efforts as Paul taught in 2 Timothy 2:2.

My hope is that I will inspire you, and provide basic information, so you can tell others about the Jesus Christ using media ministry.

CHRISTIANS HAVE A GREAT COMMISSION

All Christians have a responsibility to share their faith. In Matthew 28:19-20, Jesus said, "Go therefore and make disciples of all nations, baptizing them in the name of the Father and of the Son and of the Holy Spirit, teaching them to observe all that I have commanded you. And behold, I am with you always, to the end of the age." This passage is called "The Great Commission."

Non-Christians dislike the idea that Christians have a mandate to share their faith. They would rather Christians keep their beliefs private. In trying to mute Christian expression, they seek to delegitimize the Christian worldview in the marketplace of ideas.

Nevertheless, all Christians have an obligation to speak the truth in love. Jesus reminds us that "No one after lighting a lamp puts it in a cellar or under a basket, but on a stand, so that those who enter may see the light" (Luke 11:33).

Christian writers have a special obligation to be "salt and light" (Matthew 5:13-16) in our decaying and dark world.

Some people may speak to their neighbor about Christ and others may travel the world sharing their faith. That's good. But many can start a blog to reach the world with the message of Christian hope.

LITERATURE MINISTRY CHANGES LIVES

Our faith began with what is known as the "oral tradition." Jesus never wrote anything we know of expect a few words in the sand (John 8:3-8). He spoke to people and his message transformed their hearts and minds.

As one person shared what they heard with others, faith spread. Early disciples traveled to share the message. Then, to multiply their efforts, some, like the Apostle Paul, began writing letters to the faithful. Later, people wanted to know the history of their faith and the Gospels (Matthew, Mark, Luke and John) were written, along with the Book of Acts.

The New Testament is made up of letters by Paul and others, the histories which include the words of Christ, and the prophetic book known as Revelation.

From that point on, literature ministry blossomed and the Lord blessed it.

Since then, billions of people have come to Christ, and encouraged in their faith, through the written page. Not only when Bibles were mass printed starting in the late 1600's, but through printed sermons, commentaries, theological and inspirational books, magazine articles and today through blog posts.

Writing a blog that conveys the Christian worldview, in its many facets, is a worthy way to share the Gospel. The Holy Spirit can use your writing to change lives.

❋ ❋ ❋

Writer and missionary C.T. Studd penned this truth:

Only one life, 'twill soon be past,
Only what's done for Christ will last.

It's great if you are called to travel to international destinations to share the Gospel as I once did. However, you can make an impact for Christ around the world by sharing the Good News through blogging.

You can become an influential person by sharing your Christian values, by mobilizing other Christians, and even by raising money for Christian causes.

Donald L. Hughes

: 2 :
A BLOGGING STRATEGY FOR THE 21ST CENTURY

Let me start with a true story. I shared this story with my ChristianWritingToday.com readers in a different context, but it is a cornerstone for Christian bloggers today. It sets the stage for the kind of blogging I discuss in this book.

A DAUGHTER AND HER DAD

I was working with a Christian outreach organization and a young woman wanted us to pray for her dad. She had been a Christian since he was a teenager but her father was not a believer and she wanted us to pray for him.

The young woman sought ideas from each of us about how to convince her father to receive the Lord. She was a college graduate and thought, like many people, that most come to Christ as a result of having various ideas proven to them. That is, people receive the Lord only after they have been satisfied intellectually about all sorts of questions. This includes such things as divergent as the truthfulness of the Bible, creationism, philosophical questions, historical events, theological issues—you name it. The theory is, once people hear plausible answers to their questions they will surrender intellectually and make a giant leap of faith. But is that how it works? Not normally.

NO NEED TO APOLOGIZE

There is an entire Christian discipline of answering the questions of unbelievers and it has the unlikely name of "apologetics." No, that doesn't mean Christians are sorry for their faith. The term "apologetics" comes from the Greek word *apologia*, which means, "to defend." Apologetics is the task of defending beliefs and answering critics.

As important as apologetics may be in colleges and universities, I personally don't think it's important in families, churches or the marketplace where we normally engage friends and acquaintances, coworkers and strangers with the reality of the living Christ. Arguments—even high-minded ones—drive people away from faith.

In fact, that's what I said to the young Christian woman at the staff Bible study. I suggested she not try to prove the existence of God or to answer her father's intellectual questions. I suggested that instead she look into her father's eyes, hold his hand, squeeze it gently, and say, "I don't want to go to heaven without you daddy. Won't you please ask Jesus into your life?"

You see, most people don't become Christians because they believe the Bible is true or because someone has beat them down with intellectual arguments. Yes, I'm sure there are some exceptions to that. And I know some Christians believe that all their talk of Creationism and proof of Hell and other pet doctrines is "contending for the faith." However, this approach yields negative reactions for a reason that the Bible itself describes. It says: "The natural person does not accept the things of the Spirit of God, for they are folly to him, and he is not able to understand them because they are spiritually discerned" (1 Corinthians 2:14).

CONNECT, THEN POINT THE WAY

People come to Christ because they have a spiritual yearning that they want to satisfy. We don't need to be in a mode where we are always viciously defending the faith. Yes, there is a time for I suppose, but almost all the time we must share our lives and remember, as the old hymn reminds us:

> *Softly and tenderly Jesus is calling*
> *Calling for you and for me*

"Contending" becomes an option of last resort if we realize that all humans have a spiritual yearning. As we read the New Testament, we see that most people went to Christ out of their emotional needs rather than expecting Jesus to satisfy their intellectual curiosity. The story of the woman at the well is one of many examples of that. If you want to reach people Jesus style—in your personal life or via a blog—study that encounter in John 4.

It's worth noting that Jesus did not traffic in intellectualism at all. He spoke in parables— mysterious little stories that touch the hearts of people and cause them to think about spiritual things.

It's true Paul and some of the other apostles debated with pagans and philosophers in Athens and elsewhere. Yet, people do not generally come to Christ because with intellectual debate. Individuals come to Christ because they see the futility of their own life and they realize they need to be rescued from their sin. Most people don't have the interest or education for rigorous apologetic debate, yet everyone has a yearning to be one with God and with others.

Thus, when we share Christ with others, we need to approach them on a personal level. One based more on emotion rather than intellect. We want to approach them warmly as Christian people, not in fiery theological debate. No, I'm not suggesting for a moment that we should engage in cheap emotionalism, but I am saying we need to connect with people at their point of need. Often that is based on the events in their lives and how they feel about them.

This is a foundational idea. You want to share your interests and your life in your blog. Be an attractive Christian regardless of your topic, and be a beacon that draws people to Christ. Your blog can be on any topic you choose—one that is attractive to a wide audience—and then let your readers see Christ shine through you.

You can do that in meaningful but subtle ways. You want to be comfortable sharing your faith in a natural way.

BUILD RELATIONSHIPS

The key benefit of a blog like this is that it enables you to build a relationship with your readers. In fact, that is the whole point of this strategy.

You can share your Christian convictions through the topic you have chosen to blog about, and people can respond in your comments section. You can carry on a dialogue with them there. Normally, you can also contact them via email for private conversations.

If you're blogging for Jesus you want to build rapport and trust.

PEOPLE CHOOSE TO READ YOUR BLOG

Blogs make it easy to engage new readers. You don't have to go out and find people—search engines bring people to you.

Potential readers decide to click on the search engine link that takes them to your site. There is no coercion. People arrive at your site by an act of their free will.

I don't mean to say that when you start a new blog that people will flock to it. It's not that easy. There is an art and science called Search Engine Optimization (SEO) and you should optimize each post you write. When you do, it appears near the top of search results for certain key words you target.

SEO is not rocket science. There are free tools you can use if you follow my hosting suggestions in a later chapter. Take a few extra minutes to enter data before your post goes public, and you increase your chances of being seen.

REACH OTHERS IN CONTEXT

As a young Christian, I often went out with a team to Central Avenue in Phoenix, Arizona to share my faith. Teens were out cruising in their cars, in the great American tradition, and other teens parked along Central to watch the informal parade and to socialize.

Our team moved from car to car talking to the small groups gathered around them. Looking back, I can't say it was a very effective way to people with the Gospel. The teens were focused on other things. It was difficult to get their attention in that carnival atmosphere. The boys had lots of fun baiting us to impress their girlfriends. Yet, occasionally we were able to break through the barriers and reach individuals on a personal basis.

It's important to share the Gospel in public. However, I think it is far more important to share with people in the context of their own lives. People are more willing to hear about Jesus when they're facing some personal crisis like financial or marital calamity or the death of a loved one. Their barriers fall.

* * *

You want to build rapport so you can be there for people when the barriers are down. Rapport is defined as, "a close and harmonious relationship in which the people or groups concerned understand each other's feelings or ideas and communicate well." A blog enables you to build rapport with people.

: 3 :
BLOGGING BASICS

A blog is different than any other kind of website. In the earliest days of the Internet, people shared their lives on a daily basis in public journals. They were like diaries. Today, we see the same thing happening, in smaller snippets, on Facebook.

The first journals were called "web logs," and that evolved into the word "blog." Today, some people post regular videos in place of written content and these video logs are called, "vlogs."

THE GROWTH OF BLOGGING

Blogs were different from other types of websites because people were sharing the events in their lives and their feelings and on a daily or near-daily basis.

Over time, people started using blogs to promote their political and social views.

One of the most notable blogs of this type was the daily news and commentary posted by a woman named Arianna Stassinopoulos. That blog grew, and, after she married Congressman Michael Huffington, she renamed it the "Huffington Post." She sold what had once been a humble blog to AOL in 2011 for $315 million. Today, the Huffington Post continues to aggregate news and embodies blogs from a wide range of voices.

Many Christians may not be fans of the Huffington Post. However, it's a good example of how ideology spreads via blogs. The Christian worldview can and should be spread in the same way.

As Christians, we want to reach a wide audience in the personalized way that blogging offers.

When you have your own blog, you set the rules. That includes how much time you invest in it each week. I strongly suggest you stick to a schedule, but, of course, you set the schedule to fit your own needs. You gain the freedom to be a good steward of your time (Ephesians 5:16) and maintain your priorities.

ACCOUNTABLE BLOGGING OUTREACH

When you become a successful blogger, one who has many visitors, you gain influence for Christ. With that influence comes responsibility. The responsibilities include:

Speaking the truth in love. Contextualize the Gospel with the topic you have chosen and with which you share a common interest with your readers. You'll have the responsibility of being a firm, kind witness for Christ, without being preachy. You don't want to be weak in your proclamation of the faith either. You are a responsible Christian blogger when you strike a spiritually healthy balance.

Avoid confusing the Gospel with social or political opinions. Too many people think you can't be a Christian unless you hold a particular group of social or political views. That belief is not true and most people find it annoying. The Bible should inform your social and political views, not vice versa.

One of the greatest threats to the Christian faith is identification of nationalism (or a particular political party) with the cause of Christ. The Kingdom of Christ is radically different than any earthly country, and it is always bad to mix them. This mixing is called "Civil Religion" ("God and Country") and it grieves the Holy Spirit.

I'm a thankful American, but it saddens my soul when I see an American flag behind the pulpit. That's not the place for it if our true citizenship is in heaven. Displays of nationalism pollute our worship areas. Mixing symbols of the state in our thoughts and in our worship areas may well be the thing that is reducing Christian influence in our country and world.

As a Christian blogger, you must keep in mind that we are citizens of the Kingdom of God and the Lord Jesus is our ruler. We are ambassadors for Christ alone according the Bible (2 Corinthians 5:20).

Countries come and go. Today's hot-button political or social issue will be forgotten soon enough. Only the Gospel remains after cultures fade into history. Christian bloggers have a responsibility to be centered on Jesus and the Kingdom of God.

Recognize that blogging requires perseverance. You should be willingly accept that responsibility if you are going to influence people for Christ.

Blogging requires time. You should make sure you "count the cost" before you start one. An abandoned blog is a poor Christian testimony both for the blogger and for the person who stumbles upon it on the Internet.

People will only return to your blog when you update it at least twice a week with interesting content. The key to that is having a blog topic that you are passionate about. I discuss that in the next chapter. Adopt a topic that you can stay excited about.

The next aspect is that you need a constant flow of ideas about which to write. Responsible Christian bloggers are always looking for ideas. They're not afraid to ask their readers about what they'd like to know. Fresh, interesting content is mandatory. I explain about how to keep up the pace in following chapters.

No matter what techniques you may learn, you must be responsible enough to sit down and write. If you don't have that discipline, you are not going to be a happy blogger.

You have a responsibility to be patient. I was recently on a Facebook page I follow. A woman there said she had placed a Facebook ad, but saw no sales for her book on the first day. I smiled. If everyone could get instant sales by placing an ad then everyone would do it. But marketing books takes time and expertise. An advertisement on Facebook (or anywhere else) is not like a slot machine where you insert a coin and get an instant win.

Likewise, a Christian blog does not gain an instant readership. You want to build your readership over time and I discuss that later. It takes time, so you must be patient. Enjoy it when you see your number of page visits spike on certain days, but don't get discouraged when they drop on other days.

You are looking for a steady overall climb in visitor statistics and should not be overly concerned about daily fluctuations.

Once of my favorite pictures is one that shows a man in a rowboat on a lake. There are huge storm clouds behind him in the distance. The caption says, "Pray, but row for shore." That describes your role as a Christian blogger. Your responsibility is to expect God's blessing when you faithfully do the work.

* * *

There are many benefits and blessing awaiting Christian bloggers. But it requires consistent, responsible action.

In Matthew 13:23, Jesus talks about sowing and reaping. Your job is to sow the Word in the context of a topic that interests both you and prospective readers. When you patiently sow the seed, God provides the harvest.

: 4 :
HOW TO SELECT YOUR TOPIC

If you are a Christian and you like reading Christian books and websites, listening to Christian radio and watching Christian TV and movies, welcome to the club. Lots of Christians are absorbing Christian media, but not much of it is reaching the non-Christian world. That fact comes to us from a recent National Religious Broadcasters (NRB)/Lifeway Research scientific poll, as I reported in a post on ChristianWritingToday.com.

TALKING TO OURSELVES

Here are the results of the poll:

- Christian media has found a significant audience online. One in 4 Americans (25 percent) say they watch or listen to Christian programming every week on their computer, phone or tablet, according to the phone survey. An additional 5 percent tune in online monthly. One in 10 (9 percent) watch or listen online less than once a month.

- Two-thirds of Americans (67 percent) rarely or never watch Christian television.

- Those who skip church all together (94 percent) or have no religious affiliation (89 percent) rarely or never watch.

- Seven in 10 Americans (72 percent) rarely or never listen to Christian radio. They include those with no religious affiliation (94 percent) or who rarely (84 percent) or never (97 percent) attend church.

- Two-thirds (65 percent) rarely or never read Christian books.[2]

What does this mean? It means that as Christians we are just talking to ourselves. We are not using media to reach non-Christians. We are not properly using the media—including blogs—to fulfill the Great Commission of Matthew 28:19-20.

Remember, you don't need to preach. You don't need to do Bible studies. You don't need to debate. Your blog is where you share whatever topic interests you with another interested person. As a Christian, you add one dynamic—you share in a Christian context. Context is everything.

Writer Paul Shepheard said, "Writers use narratives to select from everything there is, and make contexts by putting the pieces into relation; that's what writers do, they make contexts."[3]

So, whatever topic you pursue with your blog, you are putting the pieces in the context of Christ.

Use your topic as a connecting point with others. And then you contextualize the topic so they learn about the transforming power of Jesus Christ.

BE PASSIONATE ABOUT "BOTH" TOPICS

As a Christian blogger, you are blogging about two things. First, you select a topic that interests you and is likely to interest a wide range of other people. It can be almost any topic you can imagine.

Second, you are blogging about the person and work of Jesus Christ and his transforming power in your life. It is your role to infuse that topic with Christian values based on the Bible in a non-directive way. Be subtle. Don't hit your readers over the head with preaching. Let the love and truth of Christ ooze out.

Yes, be passionate about your love of the Lord, but be "wise as a serpent and harmless as a dove" (Matthew 10:16). Don't scare off non-believers. As I said, you are not offering homilies, Bible studies or your views on particular doctrines. You'll never attract people who need Christ in their lives if you take a hard-nosed approach.

You must be passionate about the topic you intend to blog about—the topic that will attract reader *and* about the transforming power of Jesus Christ.

In educational theory, this method is "taking students from the known to the unknown." You start with people in familiar territory ("where they are"), then, with that foundation, take them to new levels of understanding. You are taking your blog readers from "the known"—the topic that interests them and causes them to visit your blog—to "the unknown," salvation that is only available through Jesus Christ.

Is it unethical to have a stealthy approach? Not at all. The Apostle Paul put it this way: "I have become all things to all people so that by all possible means I might save some" (1 Corinthians 9:22).

HOW TO PICK A TOPIC

Picking a topic to blog about may be easier than you think. Put your mind in neutral and ask yourself what subjects you care about.

If a topic doesn't pop immediately into your mind, I'd suggest that you think back on your education. What school subjects did you like best? Is there a work-related topic that interests you? How about your hobbies?

Here's a 300 plus list of hobbies that might spark your thinking. It has everything from Aircraft Spotting to Zumba:

NotSoBoringLife.com/list-of-hobbies/

Any of them could be a great topic for your new blog. Pick just one and start writing blog posts on the different aspects of that topic.

The only missing ingredient is your enthusiasm. Don't pick a topic if you are lukewarm about it. Do some research about the possibilities and then make a commitment.

Of course, you want to put the Lord at the forefront of your decision-making process. Pray and ask him for direction. You can and should have a conviction from the Lord about blogging on a particular topic.

MASTERY IS NOT REQUIRED

You may think you don't know enough about a topic to write 104 posts per year. Don't worry about that. Take one day at a time (Matthew 6:34).

You don't need mastery of the topic to start. What you do need is an insatiable curiosity about it.

We live in a wonderful time in history and there is information at your fingertips. You can research any topic on the Internet. You can learn new things quickly at no cost.

That doesn't mean you should cut and paste content from other sites. You must read multiple sources, process the information in your mind, combine it with your own experiences and produce something unique. I discuss the process in detail in the next chapter.

The information is out there if you are excited enough to get it. Read, watch, listen and grow.

* * *

Pick a topic that you are enthusiastic about. Make sure your choice is not rash. Consider how you'll feel about the topic a few years into the future.

Get confirmation from the Lord that you have selected the right topic. Then learn and become a thought leader on the topic. Integrate your faith into all aspects of the topic.

: 5 :
AN OVERVIEW OF THE WRITING PROCESS

Franklin D. Roosevelt said, "The only limit to our realization of tomorrow will be our doubts of today."

And what produces doubts more than anything? Fear of the unknown. I want to help remove some of that fear by giving you an overview of the writing process before you write your first post.

THE BIG PICTURE

Get a Post Idea. The first step is to know in advance what want to say. Don't leave it to a sudden last minute brainstorm.

Research and Outline. When you know a lot about the subject of your blog and topic of a particular blog post, your research requirement may be minimal. You can write what you know. However, you add depth and quality when you do some research and add quotations, statistics, and anecdotes from others or extra material that will enrich the reader experience.

Even when your head is filled with what you want to write, do a quick outline. These are just headings really, but they help you present the content in a logical way.

Write. This is the stage when you capture your ideas and put them in tangible form on the page.

Most new writers fail at this point. They think they must agonize over the creation of each sentence and paragraph. Fact: Creation is a right brain activity. Write what you have to say as quickly as possible without any thought for structure, grammar or need for perfection.

Do you know how they used to drill for oil? A wildcatter set up a derrick in a likely place and drilled. Nothing happened if it was a dry hole. But if there was oil below the ground there, drilling would reach it. There would be a rumble and then what was known as a "gusher." The oil shot out of the ground and high into the air like a fountain. The oil workers conserved the yield by capping off the well and putting one of those rocking horse pumps on it.

This is an illustration of the writing process. At this stage you let your ideas gush from your mind without any limitation. This is your first draft.

Revise. After the gush you "cap off the well" by revising what you have written.

Revision is a left-brained activity. This is the time to consider what your right brain has created and change it. You may add sentences and cut others. You may rearrange paragraphs. You make better word choices. Most of all, you will add clarity to what you gushed on the page.

New writers fail because they do not understand the distinction between writing and revision. They are totally different steps that require different thought processes. You stunt your creativity and weaken the overall quality of your final article when you try to revise as you write. Write first, then revise.

Edit. This is the step where you check your grammar, spelling, punctuation and formatting. This type of editing is called "copy editing."

Learn how to edit your own work or hire an editor. One tip is to hire a professional editor to copy edit your first 4-5 posts. Carefully study the changes the editor made. You learn from your mistakes.

There are many online sources that will help you learn to edit your own writing.[4]

Publish. This part is easy if you use WordPress as I suggest. You simply paste your article into the interface, make you headings bold, and then click the publish button or schedule it for publication at a date and time you choose. I discuss scheduling post in a later chapter.

But don't press that publish button too quickly. You have one final step to complete before you do that.

Proofread. Sadly, many people do not understand the distinctions between editing and proofreading. Copyediting is checking for consistency and accuracy. Proofreading is verifying that the copy-edited version is the one that gets published.[5]

Sometimes "gremlins" sneak in at the last moment and you can catch them in this distinct proofreading step. Never let a proofreader edit your work. You don't want someone who bills themselves as an "editor/ proofreader." Professionals know the difference and don't do both.

Notice that writing a blog post, like all writing, embodies several steps. "Write" is just one of them.

TWO COMMON QUESTIONS

The two most common questions I get about writing are: "How many words should a blog post be?" and "How long should it take me to write it?"

I used to tell people that 500 words was the sweet spot for a blog post. That's long enough to address the issue at hand, but short enough to retain reader interest.

However, longer form posts are becoming popular. Make 500 words the minimum. The best length is between 750 and 1500 words, both for readers and for Google to give your work search page ranking.

As I have said, the key to longer form writing is pithy sub-heading. People see those sub-heading and it motivates them to keep reading.

How much time should it take you to write 750 words of solid, interesting helpful information? When you try to write without preparation, expect to spend hours. If you prepare by doing initial research and a rudimentary outline as I've suggested, you'll be writing the same post in about 30 minutes.

* * *

With this overview of the writing process, you are now ready to create individual posts. There is joy in creating life-changing posts.

Donald L. Hughes

: 6 :
HOW TO CONSTRUCT A BLOG POST

There is a formula to writing a blog post. I'm going to share it with you now. However, within the confines of that formula you have one overarching obligation: You must be interesting.

Your purpose is not just to offer information. It is to engage your readers. That means you want to grab their attention, keep them reading though your entire post, and then motivate them to respond in a positive way to your call to action.

This process is not mysterious. You can do certain thing to grab the attention of readers and then sustain it. Writers use these techniques regular when they write blog posts.

Let's look at the steps to create an interesting and effective blog post.

ARTICLE COMPONENTS

Each blog post follows the same pattern. When you follow it, your posts will be more interesting and helpful to your readers. You'll also find you can write them faster when you follow this blueprint.

HEADLINE

Headline writing is a special skill, but one you can master. Write a headline for your blog post that is short, to the point and catchy. Never try to explain the content of your post in your headline. A headline is just a hook.

What kind of headlines do people click on when they see them in search results? There has been lots of research in this area. Whenever possible, use these words as part of your headline:

- How to
- Numbers (like "5 Ways to ...")
- Free
- You
- Tips
- Best
- Tricks
- Great

INTRODUCTION

Start with a relevant story. This may come from your own experience or something you read or heard. Lacking that, start your post with a question or a quotation. When you do this, you immediately seize reader attention and that's something you want to do.

Never start a post with a Bible verse. Many Christian writers think that's a spiritual thing to do. It's not. There may be a Scripture reading at church, but a blog post should never be a sermon. Sermons are vinegar to most people and you want to offer honey. Use Bible passages with appropriate, but keep them short and use them wisely and sparingly. Most non-Christians will not read your blog post if it starts with a Bible passage.

RESEARCH

Follow your introduction with research. Present interesting facts on the topic of your post. For example, if your blog is about gardening and your post is on roses, you might tell your readers the Juliet rose is valued at $5 million dollars.[6] That may be a factoid rather than a full-fledged fact, but it garners interest and launches you into your content. Needless to say, your research must be relevant to the point you're making in your post.

When you do a little research, you'll probably find other interesting tidbits. Sprinkle them throughout your post.

PRACTICAL POINTS (HEADINGS)

When you are writing a post, you generally want to make one big point that is supported by three or four sub-points which are sub-headings. You maintain the flow from introduction to research to practical points.

Your points are the heart of your article. It's where you convey your key ideas.

Headings identify each practical point with a heading. They are very short sentences or sentence fragments that are a preview of coming attractions of the following section. They serve a dual purpose. They help clarify your points and they provide an incentive for readers to keep on reading.

CONCLUSION (CALL TO ACTION)

Summarize what you what you have said. You don't repeat it, you glean and restate the main points you want people to remember. Sometimes you want to conclude with a brief story or practical application.

The best conclusions have a call to action. That's where you tell your readers what you expect them to do to make use of the idea or ideas you shared in the post.

Let me give you a biblical example of a call to action. In John 8, we have the story of a woman caught in adultery. He spoke to the accusers and the crowd. He even wrote something on the ground. What was his call to action for the woman? Jesus said, "Go, and sin no more."

You want to trigger action. Regardless of your topic, that is the main purpose of being a Christian blogger.

BLOG STRUCTURE SUMMARY

Title. It should be short, catchy, and relevant and include SEO key works when possible.

Introduction. A short, pertinent, engaging story. Hook the reader immediately.

Heading - Practical Point 1 - Make your point in a few paragraphs. Try to use 300 words or less under each heading.

Heading - Practical Point 2

Heading - Practical Point 3

... as many points as you need.

Conclusion (call to action).

Go to ChristianWritingToday.com to see a large number of examples of this structure. This simple structure will arrest reader interest and keep them reading to the end.

※ ※ ※

Every writer must overcome is inertia. That is the greatest challenge. The dictionary definition identifies the problem precisely. Inertia is, "a tendency to do nothing or to remain unchanged."

Thinking about writing is not writing. Staring at a computer screen is not writing. You must start tapping the keys. The words that appear may not say what you mean, but once you have words down, you can revise them. That is the redemptive aspect of writing. You can always change and improve what you have written.

: 7 :
SCHEDULING POSTS

You have promised your readership a post every Monday and Thursday.

But it's late Sunday night and you are sitting in the glow of your computer screen. You aren't typing. You are staring at your blank screen as if in a trance.

What's happening here? Writer's block? No. You are the victim of poor planning. You failed to schedule your writing sessions and your posts.

Scheduling your work may seem like a small thing, but it can make a huge difference in your effectiveness as a Christian blogger.

You can solve this problem by doing three things:

- Keep a running list of topics you want to write about in the future.
- Protect your writing time.

- Schedule your posts for automated release.

This plan eliminates the desperation that many bloggers feel as a result of poor planning.

KEEP A BLOG TOPIC LIST

Some writers sit down to write and hope an idea will suddenly pop into their mind. These kind of writers are called "pansters" because they are "writing by the seat of their pants."

This term was first used at the dawn of the aviation era. The first pilots had no experience or ability (no one did), so they tried to learn and survive through intuition. That was called "flying by the seat of your pants." Many writers see the ability to do this as a virtue, but I see it as a vice. Writers are far more productive when they plan their work, usually with an outline, and let their intuition kick in after you have established your main ideas.

So, I strongly recommend that you work to a plan. That starts with gathering ideas for blog posts well in advance of sitting down to write. There are lots of ways to do that, from always having a pen and writing pad handy to using computer tools like OneNote or EverNote.

Capture ideas when you come across them or when they come to mind. I have several blogs and I have ideas for posts that stretch 6-8 months into the future. I'm never at a loss about what to write.

Besides writing down the idea, I also do a tentative 3-5 point outline. Each point is made up of just a few words, sometimes a whole sentence. It adds substance to the idea. Previously, I wrote down just the idea, but I would come back to it later and wonder, "What in blazes did I mean by that?" My warehouse of ideas, with rudimentary outlines, is a valued resource that fuels my creativity.

As you can guess, having plenty of ideas allows me to write well in advance of publication dates. I don't worry about staring at a blank computer screen at the last minute. I keep my writing process on a schedule.

SCHEDULE YOUR WRITING TIME

Part of scheduling your posts is protecting your writing time. No matter if you write your posts months ahead or the day before publication, you want to maintain an independent writing schedule.

You will see your productivity and the quality of your writing increase if you do that.

How do you protect your writing time?

You must set a time to write, of course. Pick a day and time. Stick to it. I have worked with many hundreds of writers through the years and I can say that, as a class of people, they are among the worst excuse-makers that ever walked the planet.

Am I being unkind? I hope you don't see it that way. I have worked with many promising writers who squandered their vision because something always got in the way of writing. I sincerely hope that doesn't happen to you. Some excuses were more plausible than others, but the fact is they were all excuses.

Your commitment to the Lord, and to yourself, is to sit down at the appointed time and write. No excuses. It may take effort to fend off all the distractions, but that's exactly what you must do. You must protect your writing time.

Let me give you a few tips that will help you to do that.

First, it's best to have full, exclusive access to your own computer. If you're sharing a computer with your spouse or children, you will inevitably find it being used during your writing time. Also, when others use your computer, your files are at risk. It's devastating if you lose all your research or posts-in-progress.

You don't need a very powerful computer to write or access the Internet. Good laptops for this dedicated purpose sell for about $250 on Amazon.com, so it's a worthwhile investment.

Should you try to write on a tablet? Some people do. However, I've tried and I find a tablet to be a barrier to creativity. I want the flexibility to type, do research and access my blog with minimum effort. Tablets don't currently meet those requirements.

Second, have a place to write. I've found that I can write anywhere. But to do to my best, I need one crucial tool. It's called a door. I need to be able to close the door and write without distractions and interruptions.

To me, that's the ideal situation and I recommend it. You don't need to cloister yourself away for hours on end, but you do need kind of privacy that enables you creative juices to flow.

Interestingly, many people like to write in a Starbucks or other coffee shops. There is no privacy and there is human activity all around. Yet, they are able to sit in the corner with their laptop and submerge themselves into singularity of purpose.

Why do some writers find a coffee shop a comforting place to write? It eliminates the loneliness they sometimes feel, yet intrusion into their "space" is minimal. For those who want to experience the ambience without the risk of coffee jitters, there's a web site that allows you to play the background sound at home.[7]

Regardless of the place you choose, make sure you can use it during the time you have set for yourself. Consistency of writing time and place is an important part of your overall scheduling strategy.

USE THE SCHEDULING FEATURE

One of the things that makes WordPress a superior blogging platform is its ease of use. I provide details about why it is the best way to blog in a later chapter.

One of its many features is a scheduling function. You can input your post and then schedule it for a future date and time.

For example, I write posts in advance and drip feed them. At the moment, my written posts appear on ChristianWritingToday.com on Mondays at 1 AM and my video posts appear on Thursday at 1 AM. No, I don't get up at 1 AM and post them. I add them after I write and edit each post. I check my calendar and pick a future date. I set it and forget it. The post appears automatically at the scheduled time.

At the moment I have seven weeks of articles and four weeks of videos scheduled. I just keep writing posts and scheduling them. I have no "midnight stress" trying to write and publish a post at the last minute. Also, it is comforting having posts shielded in case I get sick or am away on a trip.

※ ※ ※

We generally apply 1 Corinthians 14:40 in a limited way. It only comes up in regard to chaos in a local church. That is the context, of course, but Paul's thought has a wider importance and impact. The verse says, "Everything should be done in a fitting and orderly way."

Think how that might apply to all aspects of your daily life. To family life, child-rearing and work.

It certainly applies to do writing blog posts and scheduling them on a regular basis.

Benjamin Franklin said, "Failing to plan is planning to fail." That truth of that statement has been shaped on the anvil of human experience.

Scheduling your entire blog work-flow can have a positive impact and your blogging success.

… : 8 : …
HOW TO BUILD A READERSHIP

The not-so shocking truth: There is a lot of similar content on the Internet. Since this is the case, why do some bloggers build a big readership and others do not?

In my view, it's the personality of the blogger. God has given you a unique personality and you need to let it shine though in your writing. Your post content may be similar to posts by others, but your personality, which includes your experiences and insights, makes your writing unique.

Your unique perspective is key to building your readership. But there are other important elements you must add to that. Here are four key things you can do to build your readership.

UNDERSTAND THE SEO WORLD

There's an old joke among bloggers. It goes like this:

Question: "Where is the best place to hide a dead body?"

Answer: "Page 2 of Google search results."

The point is, people searching for content only view results on the first page. They seldom go to page 2 of the results. Google may report "975,000 results in 0.44 seconds" at the top of each search results page, but that statistic is meaningless.

You get lots of free "traffic" when your post appears on the first page for a search term that people are using to find content. This way of building a readership is called the "organic search" method and it's an important one.

How do you get on the first page of a Google research and benefit from all the free visitors you'll get when people click your link? Well, that's an art and science called Search Engine Optimization (SEO).

You get page ranking by a combination of factors. One factor is that posts must embody the same key words or phrases in your title, headings and content. That makes it easy for Google to filter your content.

So, when the key word (or phrase) you use strategically throughout a particular post matches the words that people type into the Google search box, your blog post link is likely to appear on the first page of Google or other search engine.

For example, I have a post on ChristianWritingToday.com called, "How Many Words Make a Book?" If you do a Google search, you'll see it shows on the first page. I wrote it in 2010 and it has had high ranking since then. Tens of thousands of people have visited ChristianWritingToday.com over the years since then because of that ranking. And people usually stick around to read my other posts.

You must embody key words or phrases that are relevant to your blog post to benefit from organic search. However, you cannot "keyword stuff" because Google doesn't like that and will put that post on page 1,237 (or deeper) if they think you are trying to rig search results. Their search algorithm can tell. It's best to pick a key word or phrase and repeat it 4-5 time in different parts of your post.

If you use WordPress (from WordPress.org, not WordPress.com) you can simplify all this by using the free Yoast SEO plug-in.[8] It is easy to use and it gives you a fighting chance for a high search page ranking.

Your blog posts will get higher search engine rankings when other sites link to it. That proves to the Google "spider," which periodically indexes your site, that your content is important to other readers. Google and other search engines like to please searchers by putting high quality content at the top of their results.

Link-building takes time and is one of those things you do over time. There are many places online to learn how to do it.[9]

Yes, it's true that people will link to particular posts automatically if your content is helpful and interesting. However, you doing back-linking is part of your continuing site promotion. It's necessary to do, but you do it over time.

Link to particular blog posts, not just to your home page. That makes the link more valuable to you.

I have a warning for you about back-linking. NEVER pay someone to do it. You need high quality back-links, not links from spammy sites. You need links from relevant sites on the same or similar topic as your site. Those who offer "5,000 back-links for $5" (or any number at any price) are not doing careful linking. Google will actually lower your page ranking for your site, or for individual posts, if they see incoming links from sites they have identified as being spammy.

So, learn more about how to use key words and phrases and back-linking. You'd get lots of free traffic when you take the time to get visibility in this way.

USE SOCIAL MEDIA

Social media can be helpful to build your readership. You should have a least a Facebook page and Twitter account for your blog. Never use your personal accounts. Establish new accounts so you can promote just your blog.

The more people you get on your Facebook or Twitter accounts, the more effective you can be in promoting your blog. However, don't make these methods your life. For example, whenever a new post appears on ChristianWritingToday.com, news about it automatically appears on both my CWT Facebook and Twitter accounts.

Occasionally I go to each account and interact with people, but I know the secret of social media, so I don't allow it to take too much of my time.

What is that secret? It's this: You ALWAYS use social media to drive traffic TO your blog. You NEVER use your blog to drive readers to your social media pages.

If you have a Facebook "Like" button on your blog, people go to your Facebook page. Other than offering social proof, that's a dead-end street. It offers you little or no readership building benefits. You want a "Share" button. That way, your blog visitors share a post they like on their page and all their friends see it. That process of multiplication is what builds your readership.

The same is true with Twitter. It may be nice to have 10,000 followers, but gathering them on your blog is counter-productive. Enable readers to Tweet about your post to all their followers to get a chain reaction effect going. That's how you build a readership.

So, use social media wisely. Allocate time each week to promoting your blog, but in my view do not spend more than 15% of that time on social media.

DO ONLINE NETWORKING

One of the most effective ways to build your readership is through online networking.

No, I'm not talking about joining Linkedin or one of those sites. I'm suggesting you build a relationship with like-minded people—other Christian bloggers or general bloggers in your topic area.

You don't use fancy Internet-era techniques; you use old-fashioned friendship-making techniques. Show interest in the work of others. Encourage them. Share ideas. Offer help. Many good things will grow out these types of relationships.

Yes, it is nice if you could meet these people in-person, but we now have the possibility to build deep, meaningful, mutually beneficial relationships online. It happens via email, chat and maybe even video Skype calls where you can see each other as you talk.

Just show your genuine Christian concern for others and you will form many satisfying bonds. God will bless these relationships. You'll discover that others will want to help you build your readership and you will want to help them build their readership.

Throw your net of friendship as wide as possible. It is worthwhile to do.

CREATE A MAILING LIST

I have saved this for last because it is probably the most important way to build your readership. Once people find you through SEO or other means, you want to conserve your results. You do that by collecting the first name and email address of your visitors.

They will gladly give you this information if you offer them something they want. Not only do you offer an email newsletter, but you give them a bonus to motivate them to sign up.

What kind of bonus should you offer? It depends on the topic of your blog. Generally, you want something in digital format so people can sign-up and download the bonus immediately. So, a short ebook on some interesting aspect of your topic may entice them. You normally offer it in PDF format.

Creating a mailing list is not difficult. There are many services you can use like MailChimp.com, GetResponse.com or aWeber.com. They all simplify and automate the entire sign-up and newsletter delivery process. I have tried them all and personally I like MailChimp.com best. You can build your list to 2,000 subscribers before you start paying for their service.

Should you ask for more than a first name and email address? Studies have shown people willingly give you this, but are reluctant to give more, like a last name. They certainly don't want to give you their address or phone number in almost all cases.

How often should you send your newsletter? You can send a regular newsletter on a monthly basis or you can send one every time you add a post. Give people an idea of what they're signing up for when you collect their data. You never want to spam them with unwanted material. Some people will unsubscribe if they don't like what you're sending, and that's okay.

You increase your readership and sphere of influence when you have a mailing list. You want to grow it to be as large as possible. Also, if you have products and services related to your blog topic, you can offer them to the people on your mailing list. They are your most dedicated followers and you'll get your best response from them.

* * *

Promoting your blog is a never-ending process. You can't do it once and forget it. Some successful bloggers dedicate at least 2-3 hours per week (more in the beginning) to get visibility.

Become aware of the many different ways to build your readership. I have offered four methods to get you started, but there are hundreds of techniques. Not only that, old methods become less useful over time and new methods emerge. You must stay abreast of trends.

You want to write blog posts that capture reader interest. But you need to let people know your blog exists. Never-ending promotion is the way to build your readership.

… : 9 : …
INCOME OPTIONS

If you see your blog as a ministry, is it right to expect an income from it?

There is no question about that. Jesus said, "...the laborer deserves his wages" (Luke 10:7). The Apostle Paul reiterated the same idea in 1 Timothy 5:18: "You shall not muzzle an ox when it treads out the grain... The laborer deserves his wages."

You can be a volunteer blogger, but I don't recommend that. You will have expenses you'll need to cover. Also, your time is valuable and you deserve compensation according to the Bible passages I've mentioned. You may want to make Christian blogging a full-time ministry if God blesses your work, so developing an income stream from the beginning can be important.

Tracking both visitors and income is motivational. You can see God's blessing in a tangible way.

There is nothing spiritual about working for free. If you don't need the money, I suggest you develop income sources and give profits to your local church or other Christian ministry.

There are two keys to receiving an income from your blog. One is site visitors (traffic). The more traffic you have, the greater your potential of making money. Second, a successful blog requires superior content in the form of your blog posts. Visibility for your writing comes through site promotion. Never pass up an opportunity to promote your blog in ways large and small.

Here are some monetization methods that work.

MARKET YOUR OWN PRODUCTS OR SERVICES

If you have a blog that reaches a large audience, you can offer your own products or services.

Of course, if you're blogging for Jesus, make sure your product or service is compatible with the message and tone of your blog.

You must know your audience to determine what they might buy. You may think you can sell icicles to Inuits, but they would probably prefer insulated undies.

For example, you may have written a book or ebook. That is usually easy to sell. I discuss that in a later chapter.

Books you have written can be on any topic as long it is in keeping with the overall ministry goals of your blog. For example, if you

Christian blog is about gardening, and you extol God's creation, you can offer a wide range of products or services that relate to that focus.

People are eager to take online courses, so if you know how to produce them, you can support your blog, and perhaps your family, by offering relevant, helpful, interesting instructional materials. More about that later.

Your blog is about Christian values and how they apply in a specific area of life. Your ability to create products and services grows when you stop and think about the larger implications of what you're trying to convey.

As I've said before, a Christian blog is not a pulpit. You are not hammering people with Bible teaching. You are using a specific topic to "woo" them to Christ or to help them live more meaningful Christ-centered lives if they are already Christians.

So, relevance is the first rule. Offer your own products and services only if they are relevant to the mission of your blog.

The second rule, and the only other really important one, is that you don't want to seem like your blog exists only to promote your products or services. Balance is required between telling people about what you have to offer and what is known as the "hard sell." You want to avoid that, of course. Offer your products and services by highlighting benefits and giving a call to action.

You don't want to sell or over-sell in a way that others might consider offensive. You can do that best when you help people understand the benefits of what you're offering.

Keep the central focus of your blog in mind when you write posts. Selling your own products and services is important, but secondary. Follow "best practices" for drawing people to your blog and let the Lord take care of the increase.

ADVERTISING NETWORKS

There are a large number of advertising networks. They sell the ads to customers, and you get a snippet of connecting code to put on your blog to display the advertisement.

You get paid a percentage of the ad sales price when someone clicks on the ad, which is called Pay Per Click (PPC). The other way you get paid with such ads is a small amount every time the ad is displayed. You get a proscribed amount for each thousand displays — called impressions--and is referred to as CPM.

Ad networks include Infolinks.com Media.net and Intelllinks.com among hundreds of others. However, the most popular one is Adsense, which is owned by Google.

It seems like every web site has Google ads. There's nothing wrong with that. Google makes nearly $70 billion each year from advertising, and you get a share of that when you place Adsense ads on your site.

One of the good things about Adsense is that the ads are contextualized for the most part. That is, the text in a particular article determines what ads will appear. They correlate your blog content with reader interest, and that makes it easy for you.

There is another Adsense feature that benefits Christian bloggers. The Adsense interface allows you to refuse certain types of advertising. For example, you'll be unlikely to want to display some of those lurid sexual ads or get-rich-quick schemes. Adsense allows you to refuse such ads by category.

Many of the other ad networks require you to have an established blog and a certain number of page views to be accepted into their programs. Adsense is kinder. They only care that your blog is operational.

Visit Adsense.com to learn more about the Adsense program.

AFFILIATE MARKETING

Affiliate marketing can be profitable. You sell other people's products and get a commission for doing it.

With ads, you get paid a small amount based on clicks or page impressions. With affiliate marketing, you only get paid when someone actually buys the product from the owner. The good news is that each sale may put $25 to $50 or more in your pocket.

You have to select products you think your audience will buy, but that's the hardest part. The seller provides images and links to you and delivers the product for you.

The best way to get involved as an affiliate is by going signing up at Clickbank.com. They have a huge selection of products to choose from and they offer other benefits for those who use their system. Clickbank manages affiliate programs and have systems in place to make sure you get properly paid.

There are many other affiliate programs. The Amazon program is one of the best known. If you join their program (affiliate-program.amazon.com), offer bigger ticket items ($75 or more) because the commission is tiny if you only sell books.

* * *

Remember, the more traffic you have, the higher your income will be. Getting traffic takes additional work on your part, but it could be a good use of your time. Traffic-building involves research and writing, two basic skills all writers already have.

: 10 :
HOW TO SET UP YOUR BLOG

Linda, a woman in my church wanted to encourage young moms. She had raised three girls to adulthood and each had their own family.

She saw the kinds of challenges they were facing with their families and, being the good mom she was, was always encouraging her girls.

She thought a blog would give her the opportunity to share her Christian values, relationship knowledge and practical homemaking tips with young married women.

But she made a fatal mistake at the very beginning of her blogging journey, and sadly it came to a sad end. Let me tell you about that. It is essential to lay at strong foundation at the very beginning of your blogging work.

GET STARTED RIGHT

Many new Christian bloggers are trying to get started on a budget, so they start their blog at free places like Blogger.com or WordPress.com. That was Linda's error.

Her Blogger.com account was free, but she discovered that using the assigned domain name (lindahelper.blogspot.com) she had almost no visibility.

Also, people saw it was using a free blog and that hurt her credibility.

She found the free account had all sorts of rules and she had little flexibility. They could shut down her site any time they wished.

As time when on, Linda needed to expand her online presence, but it was impossible. If she moved to an independent site with her own domain name, she would have lost all her followers and the links that led to her site.

Rather than put all the effort into rebuilding her lost following, she decided she would retire from blogging. She was disappointed, but she recognized she had made a bad decision in starting with a free site, and was forced to live with the consequences.

Later, Linda reshaped the content of her blog into an ebook, so she was able to share her love for the love and her motherly experience in that way.

MAKE AN INVESTMENT

Your biggest investment when you become a Christian blogger is your time. You want to protect that investment by creating a site that has the elements you need to reach an ever-growing audience.

You want to set your own rules about what you publish, not be subject to the rules of a huge company that owns the free blogging platform that may not like your Christian values.

Some paid platforms, like Wix or Squarespace, are little better. They are not free, but the appeal is that they are easy to set up. However, you must still comply with their Terms of Service and Acceptable Use Policy and if you don't, they'll shut you down and you'll lose all your hard work. Their documentation is sufficiently broad that they can take action against you if you say anything of a political, social or theological nature with which they disagree.

I'm not suggesting that Christian bloggers are out to break the rules. That's not the point. I'm only suggesting that you retain your independence in our turbulent times. No matter what the topic of your blog, you want to speak the truth in love. But often corporations don't see it the Christian way. It is best to have your own independently hosted blog where you set the rules.

To do that, you must set up your own web site at the very start. I would go so far to say that if you are not willing to do that, then it's probably best to not waste your time as a blogger. Find another way to honor the Lord.

How much will an independent site cost to set up? $50 is probably enough to get you started.

5 STEPS TO SETTING UP YOUR BLOG

My strongest recommendation is that you set up you own independent blog on hosting. Why?

- You retain control.
- You have your own Terms of Service.
- You can say pretty much what you wish.
- You can use many different methods to build traffic.
- You can make money with ads and no one will interfere with your efforts.

1. BUY A DOMAIN NAME

Choose carefully because this is your "brand." Should it be our name? Should it include the topic of your blog? How long or short should the domain name be?

If your name is available, that might be a good choice as long as your name isn't Hubert Blaine Wolfeschlegelsteinhausen. In my case, DonaldHughes.com was being used by another good-looking guy with my name, so I settled for DLHughes.com.

Would I have used DonaldLHughes.com if available? No. Initials in the middle of a name often confuse people. People are less likely to remember the "L" and may end up at another site.

If your name is Betty and your blog topic is gardening, then "GardeningByBetty.com" might be a good choice.

Also use a "dot com," never a "dot net" or other domain name type. Not using "dot com" may make you invisible because it is the standard, expected extension.

Never accept a "free" domain name from anyone. They will own it, not you. You want a domain name you can register with ICANN (the regulatory agency) in your own name.

Be careful of those "$1.99 the first year" type of offers. They are likely to charge you $39.95 for each following year. A common, fair price for a 'dot com" domain name, with no strings attached, is typically in the $10-$12 per year range right now.

Never buy your domain name from your hosting company. If you do, and have troubles, they can lock you out completely when they manage both your domain name and hosting. Keep domain name registration and hosting separate.

Buy your domain from an established, authorized company like NameCheap.com, DomainDiscover.com or another certified independent ICANN domain name seller. I've had all my domain names with DomainDiscover.com for 17 years now and am happy with their price and service.

I would never advise anyone, under and circumstances, to buy a domain name from either GoDaddy.com or Register.com.

2. GET DOMAIN HOSTING

This is the server where you site resides in cyberspace. You're renting space on a computer that connected to the Internet infrastructure and anyone anywhere can reach your site when they type in your domain name.

There are many affordable hosting plans at places like 1and1.com or HostGator.com. They have good plans that are $5-$15 per month, but you can usually get a cheaper rate if you sign up for an annual plan.

Again, I want to warn you about GoDaddy.com. They are cheap, but are not recommended for a number of reasons.

3. INSTALL WORDPRESS ON YOUR HOST

There are several ways to do this.

- You can go to WordPress.ORG (not WordPress.com) and get instructions there.
- Many hosts like 1and1.com and have one-click WordPress installation and that works well.

- You can hire a web person to create your site for you. I have had my own author website/blog installation service for over a decade. If you want to use my low cost service, visit VelocityWriting.com/author-platform-websites/ for details. I offer value for money because you get a basic site you can start using immediately, plus 30 days of free support to help you master your blog. I don't abandon my clients. Yes, that was a shameless plug. And you may want to see my many other personalized author services on that site. But feel free to explore other options.

- Also, feel free to do it yourself. It can be a new, fun experience for you. You can and should install WordPress yourself if you're the adventurous type. It's not overly complex. Also, you can get support from your hosting company when you install WordPress from your hosting account. There are so many good tutorials on YouTube.com and elsewhere.

4. SELECT A THEME

A template determines the "look" of a WordPress blog. There are thousands of free templates available. You can also buy custom templates for $20-$60 (sometimes more) if you want a special look. A paid template is not essential when starting. You can easily switch templates later.

One of the best free and flexible templates for blogs is called Hueman.[10] It's simple to change Hueman elements to give your blog a unique look. Secret: I use the Hueman template (paid version) on ChristianWritingToday.com. What you see there is just one of many dozens of possible configurations.

There is a major caution when it comes to the "look" of your blog. That is, don't get hung up on a fancy-looking blog with lots of bells and whistles. Too many new bloggers spend far too much time (and money) trying to make an online fashion statement. That's a waste of time and resources. The best blogs put function before fashion. Use a simple, easy to use template and adorn it with your writing, not a bunch of visual or technical doodads. Yes, add pictures, audio or videos if they enhance the posts you have written, but you want a basic blog that looks clean and does not require a lot of maintenance.

5. ADD PLUG-INS

You will soon learn that independently hosted WordPress accepts what are known as plug-ins. These are apps that you can easily install which enhance the functionality of your site. There are literally thousands of these plug-ins available, but here are six that I recommend you use from the beginning. They are all free.

A. Jetpack. This adds many different functions that you'll find useful. Use the free version, not the paid version. You'll learn that to use their tracking function you'll need to sign up with Google Analytics, which is also free. Do that because it enable you to see how many site visitors your get on a daily and monthly basis.

B. Akismet. This protects your blog from unwanted spam. The free version will meet your needs.

C. Yoast SEO. Use the free version to optimize each of your blog posts. You can enhance your page ranking on Google and other search engines. Yoast offers many support documents and you'll find it is easy to use.

D. Contact Form 7. This free plug-in allows you to easily set up a contact page. People can interact with you, but no one will be able to harvest your email address and spam you later.

E. TinyMCE Advanced. WordPress has a built-in word processor, but this plug-in adds functionally. It makes it easy to format your blog posts and to add images if you wish.

F. UpdraftPlus. This plug-in automatically backs up your entire site to the online storage place of your choice, like Dropbox.com for example. If you site ever crashes, hit by a virus or other problem, you can easily reinstall it from the backup. It's cheap insurance, especially since both the plug-in and online storage sites have free versions. The free versions are all you need.

✽ ✽ ✽

Is that all you need to know to set up your blog? No, but it's enough guidance to get you started. You will learn more as you get into it.

Keep in mind that once you set up your blog, there is little or nothing else of a technical nature you need to do. You simply write your content and post it online with a click or two.

: 11 :
USE YOUR BLOG AS A LAUNCH PLATFORM

If you are a faithful blog-builder, you'll discover that it has the power to launch you into greater ministry. As Jesus said in Luke 16:10, "Whoever can be trusted with very little can also be trusted with much." What kinds of things can happen when you're a faithful blogger? Let me offer a few suggestions.

LAUNCH AS A LEADER

Once you establish your blog you'll likely discover that others will put you in a leadership role. You may not seek it, and it is best to be a humble leader, but it is a role the Lord will want you to assume. He is putting ideas in your head so you can express them through your personality. People will react favorably and seek answers and direction from you.

Ideally, people will ask you, "What must I do to be saved?" That's always a great question that Christian bloggers love to hear. But people will come to you for answers to many questions. They may be about the topic of your blog. "What's the best carburetor to use on a short block Chevy engine?" if your blog is about hot rods. Or, "Do you advise potash for roses?" if your blog is about gardening. Name the topic and people will ask you for your opinion.

You'll also get what I call "nuts and bolts" questions. People will want to know how you set up your blog, or where you get ideas for posts, and about your writing methods. It's good when people recognize the effort you put into your blog and want to emulate you.

Other bloggers will likely recognize your efforts and ask you to write a guest blog for them. As I have said, it's great to do that to get greater exposure for your own blog. Sometimes you will ask another blogger if you can submit a guest blog, and that's okay too. They will take a look at your blog, and if you have done good work, they will be happy to work with you.

Your blog—on whatever topic—makes you an authority. You may be modest and not think so, but the old saying holds true: "In the land of the blind, the one-eyed is king."

Here's my "new blogger" paraphrase of Timothy 4:12:

> *Let no one despise you for your knowledge when you're just starting out. But be an example to believers and unbelievers alike in your writing, speech, conduct, love, and faith. Share your topic and your faith in purity of heart.*

If the Lord uses you and your blog to inform and inspire others, accept the mantle of leadership with grace. The Lord has plans for you. You the Lord when you expand your Christian influence.

LAUNCH INTO BOOKS

You know what you call twelve 1,000-word blog posts on the same topic? You call it an ebook.

You know what you call three ebooks on the same topic put together? You call it a paperback book.

Once you have either, you can create an audiobook.

It's a desirable thing to repurpose your writing and sell them as book editions. You expand your leadership reach and you and have the opportunity for additional income.

New writers sometimes say, "Isn't repurposing my writing a form of plagiarism?" There is a new and growing "plagiarism industry" today. They are making money by making outrageous rules about what constitutes plagiarism. Repeated material is easy to find on the Internet, so they are out to make money by triggering fear and confusion.

These people, and some academics, will tell you that what they call "self-plagiarism" is horrid. That is part of the new wave of censorship we see so much of these days. Still, Academics give the same class lecture year after year with only minor changes.

Politicians give the same stump speech scores of time during a campaign. By plagiarism industry magnate standards, this would be self-plagiarism, but they can't make money off them.

Tell me, when Albert Einstein came up with the Theory of Relativity, should he have refrained from writing papers, books and giving lectures about it due to fear of "self-plagiarism" after releasing his original document? After all, it was the same old "$E=mc^2$" thing over and over again.

You see how absurd the plagiarism police have become? They are the same politically correct people who have formed themselves into the word police and want to limit your expression by banning certain words. Professional writers must ignore this nonsense. You want to repurpose your Christian writing and make your ideas available in as many variations and in as many mediums as possible. They can start as blog posts, but you have every right to reshape your content into any form you wish.

Let me add one more point while we're thinking about these matters. Politically correct people will tell you it's plagiarism to use other people's ideas without giving them credit. That's a bogus idea for the most part. We are all dipping into to a river of human ideas and it's a little bit crazy that anyone thinks we give credit for them. Of course, you'd want to give Einstein credit for the Theory of Relativity and not claim it is your own. But beyond unique ideas like that, you are completely free to take ideas and shape them into something unique and not feel forced to give credit to your influencers. It is a copyright violation to steal their words, but no one can copyright ideas.

Politically correct people think there is some merit in citing the source of the ideas you use. That runs counter to Judeo-Christian ethics. Christian ethics are based on the Bible. In Ecclesiastes 1:9 we read, "What has been will be again, what has been done will be done again; there is nothing new under the sun." That is a touch of reality.

Many people don't realize that Shakespeare's Romeo and Juliet was adapted, without credit, from an earlier work by Arthur Brooke. He probably got it from an old Italian tale. But since Romeo and Juliet, the tale has been recycled into other novels and plays, and films as diverse as West Side Story and Disney's High School Musical, without mentioning William. You are perfectly free to take the plot of Romeo and Juliet and shape it into something fresh and new. You do not need to credit Shakespeare.

Am I saying it's okay to take ideas and recycle them into some unique without crediting sources? Yes, I am. We are all standing on the shoulders of those who came before us. Take the best of everyone you can, and then turn that inspiration into some unique. That's how the humanity has progressed over the eons.

By the way, you'll get ideas for your blog posts from other bloggers in many cases. That's the way it works. Do you think their idea was totally original? No, they got the ideas somewhere else too. This is another example of how we are all dipping into the same river of human knowledge.

No, don't copy them. Be sure to credit direct quotes or paraphrases. But that's different than gathering ideas from others. Use others for inspiration to write something from your own unique perspective. But don't worry about providing citations about all those who influenced your thoughts. That's not necessary.

LAUNCH INTO COURSES OR PODCASTS

Your blog can also be a Launchpad into online courses and/or podcasts. Both are very popular, and you can recycle your blog posts into courses or podcasts on your topic and they will help people. You'll get paid for them and expand your sphere of influence for the Lord.

Online courses require production skills, but your blog posts can be the seeds of training about your topic. You rewrite them into a script for a visual medium. You may do "talking head" training, or you can do the visuals and the 'voice-overs" off-screen.

Podcasts are audio only. You record your rewritten posts, combining or expanding on them if you wish. You make them conversational and informative. Sometimes, you may want to do recorded telephone interviews with other experts on your topic. You add music and a fancy into, and end with music. You repurpose your writing into a different medium that will attract a different audience.

I know people who write a series of posts and reshape it into am online course. After they produce it, they extract the audio, add music and an intro, and make each lesson a podcast installment.

Later, you may write your own original scripts for online courses or podcasts, but it is perfectly acceptable to repurpose your blog posts. Recycle your work using your blog as a launch pad.

LAUNCH INTO PUBLIC SPEAKING

Many bloggers become public speakers. If you want to go that route, there are several Christian-oriented speakers' bureaus you can contact. They'll look at your blog and may want to sign you up. Not only do speaking engagements enlarge your sphere of influence for the Lord, but speaking fees can be enough over time to put your kids through college.

Not only that, but the exposure will help you get more blog visitors, book readers, blog listeners or online course students. There is nothing wrong with that. It is an expression of God's blessing in your life. You're not in it to get rich. You're in it to honor the Lord, but, as I have said, the Bible teaches, "the servant is worthy of his or her wages." Like anyone else in ministry, you deserve to get paid for your time and talents. If you're already rich, take the fee anyway and donate it to some worthy Christian cause.

Donald L. Hughes

* * *

The takeaway here is that you can blog and be blessed. Or you can use your blog as a Launchpad to greater service for the Lord. The choice is yours. However, you don't get to make that choice until you start blogging.

: 12 :
A BLESSING ON CHRISTIAN BLOGGERS

Many years ago I knelled at the front of my church. Ministers, who had earlier examined my biblical knowledge and qualifications, gathered around me and placed their hands on my head as they prayed a blessing.

This was an ordination ceremony. They were acknowledging God's call on my life, attesting that I held to sound doctrine, and providing legal status for ministry. They were setting me apart (Acts 13:2) for the work of the Gospel.

Back then, ministry was narrowly defined. You were generally commissioned as a pastor or missionary. Things have thankfully changed. People can be ordained to do a much larger range of God's work.

In my case, I have spent decades in media ministry. I believe I have seen far more fruit though that than I could have ever expected in pastoral ministry. That is one reason why I think blogging can be an important form of ministry.

THE POWER OF THE PRINTED PAGE

A person who shares the Gospel through the printed page (paper or electronic) has the same mission and authority as the person who preaches from a pulpit.

For example, the Apostle Paul was a powerful preacher, but it is his writing that remains with us today. His body of work, which total 32,400 words in the original Greek language in which he wrote, makes up 23 percent of the New Testament.

John was a preacher too, but he was also a writer. His Gospel, three epistles and the Book of Revelation make up 20 percent of the New Testament.

However, who made the biggest writing contribution to the New Testament? It was a physician (Colossians 4:14), not a preacher. Dr. Luke wrote the history of Jesus' ministry and the early church (Gospel of Luke and Book of Acts) and they constitute 27 percent of the New Testament.[11]

That is proof of the power of Christian literature. Yes, God inspired these men in a special way, but he can also inspire you in a different but meaningful way.

A BLESSING FOR YOU

Take this blessing to heart as a Christian blogger:

"For I know the plans I have for you, declares the Lord, plans to prosper you and not to harm you, plans to give you hope and a future" Jeremiah 29:11.

God gave this message to Jeremiah when the people of Israel were in captivity to the Babylonians. So, it was not delivered in the best of times, but in the worst of times.

And not only did it apply then, but it is God's message to you in the 21st century. Embrace this blessing, go forth, and spread the Good News with joy. You are empowered to bring faith and hope to the world through your blog.

You can accept this commission and this blessing on your own. However, you can also ask your pastor or a few close Christian friends to formally commission your blogging ministry. Kneel at the front of your church or in your living room, and let these people pray a blessing upon you.

The ritual of commitment and commissioning, whether public or private, will be a spiritual encouragement to you. That is your starting point for your literature ministry.

Then, through your blog, which can reach the world, you enlarge your Christian influence. Don't hold back. Do as Isaiah said: "Enlarge the place of your tent, stretch your tent curtains wide, do not hold back; lengthen your cords, strengthen your stakes" (Isaiah 54:2).

❋ ❋ ❋

Will your Christian blogging success come fast or slow? Will you stick to it for the long haul or will you get sidetracked? Will you be able to point tens of thousands to Christ or just a few?

We cannot know the precise results of our blogging efforts. We can only be found faithful doing what God has called us to do. Proverbs 16:9 provides the reality we all face. "In their hearts humans plan their course, but the Lord establishes their steps."

May God bless you as you blog for Jesus.

Did you gain benefit from this book?
Please take a moment to leave a review at Amazon.com.
Thank you.

A BIBLICAL BASIS FOR CHRISTIAN RELATIONSHIP BLOGGING

I referenced John 4 several times in this book. It is the biblical foundation of Christian relationship blogging. Let's see some spiritual and practical principles it contains for Christian bloggers.

COMMUNICATING WITH OTHERS IN A NATURAL WAY

Jesus is heading in Judea and was heading back to Galilee. Because of the geography, he went through Samaria. It was a shortcut.

Because of history, politics and a difference of religious views that went all the way back to the Babylonian captivity, the Jews and Samaritans often had hostile feelings toward each other. They avoided each other.

However, Jesus was above this pettiness. He'd go anywhere and talk to anyone.

That's the first thing we can learn about Christian relationship blogging. You are not just communicating with other Christians. You are trying to communicate with everyone.

ENGAGING OTHERS IN THEIR TERRITORY

We see that Jesus told his disciples to in the town, Sychar, bring back some lunch while he waited at the local watering hole called Jacob's Well. A woman came to the well to draw water.

That's the second thing we learn about Christian relationship blogging. We don't need to go out to a street corner and try to preach to people. They come to us. It's a lot easier to communicate with others when they come to us by their own volition.

ENGAGING OTHERS ON A NEUTRAL TOPIC

What happened next? Jesus asked her for a drink since she was there to draw water from the well.

That's the 3rd principle of Christian relationship blogging. We don't immediately start preaching. We talk about something of common interest. In this case, the topic was water. Your blog will be on some topic of general interest—a topic that will attract everyone, not just Christians. Your blog topic is something that you're passionate about—hot rods or gardening or anything else as I said before. Others will come to your blog because they share an interest in that topic.

Since you are a Christian, many of your blog posts will mention your faith in subtle ways. You can and should blend your faith into your topic in a natural way. You don't want to use Christian jargon or quote Bible verses, you want to drop your Christian like bread crumbs in a forest.

LET OTHERS RESPOND TO YOU

What happened next? The Samaritan woman asked him, "How can you, a Jew, ask for a drink from me, a Samaritan woman?" She said that because, as we know, the Jews had nothing to do with Samaritans.

The woman's simple question is rich with meaning for Christian relationship blogging. Once people come to your blog to learn more about hot rods or roses, or whatever your topic may be, they will start asking you questions of all kinds. They always do. If your faith shines through, they will eventually ask you questions about your beliefs.

If Jesus had been a blogger, his blog could have been about water. All aspects of water. Everything from rain to reservoirs. From sports hydration needs, to supplying clean water to people. Water is a huge topic, but like the Samaritan woman, people will eventually ask a question like, "Why are you interested in water?"

USE THE OPPORTUNITY TO DO GOOD

Jesus took an everyday topic like water and turned it into a conversation about spiritual truth. That's your job as a Christian relationship blogger. Turn the conversation to spiritual matters when you have the opportunity.

Notice how Jesus turned the conversation. He did not try to make some theological point. If fact, he specifically avoided that. He could have gone into a long dissertation about the doctrinal errors of the Samaritan people. Christians do that sort of thing all the time, but Jesus refused to fall into that trap.

FOLLOW THE JESUS PATTERN

- He created an opportunity to speak to someone on a neutral, non-religious topic.
- He engaged the woman as a human being with spiritual needs.
- He did not judge or condemn the woman.
- He did not preach any of his favorite doctrines.
- He spoke to the woman's personal and emotional needs.
- He revealed himself as the Messiah.

These principles will help you reach your neighbors and the world for Christ from your computer.

This is the heart of Christian relationship blogging. As a Christian blogger, your role is to, "Let your light shine before people in such a way that they will see your good actions and glorify your Father in heaven" (Matthew 5:16).

Donald L. Hughes

ABOUT THE AUTHOR

Donald L. Hughes is the editor of ChristianWritingToday.com. He is a writer, editor and publisher who has been in Christian media for over three decades.

Don has degrees from Azusa Pacific University (B.A.), Wheaton Graduate School (M.A.) and Princeton Theological Seminary (M.Div.).

Don has held several media positions over the years, including roles as an editor at Christian Life Publications where he used his skills on Christian Life magazine (later, Charisma + Christian Life), Christian Bookseller magazine (renamed Christian Retailing) and Creation House Books.

He served as Director of Communications for the educational division of the National Association of Evangelicals, and Media Director for an international faith-based organization serving at-risk children.

Don has covered stories in 31 countries as a Christian journalist. He has taught at conferences and Christian colleges both in the U.S. and overseas and was named to *Outstanding Educators of America*. He currently teaches online courses on various aspects of writing.

END NOTES

1 It's true that rural people and the poor, especially in Third World nations, may never be Internet users. They must be reached in other ways. However, there are many unbelievers in advanced countries and blogs can be an effective way to enter their world. Internet user statistics are from: http://www.internetlivestats.com/internet-users.

2 See the full article at http://www.christianwritingtoday.com /christian-media-talking-mostly-to-ourselves/

3 Shepheard, Paul. 2013. *How to Like Everything*. 1st ed. Lanham: John Hunt Publishing. p. 81.

4 For a good editing process summary, see:

https://www.themuse.com/advice/5-steps-for-editing-your-own-writing.

If you have questions about grammar or other writing-related mechanics, visit the Purdue University Writing Lab:

https://owl.english.purdue.edu/owl.

5 Where did the term "proofreading" come from? In book publishing a book underwent copy editing. Then, the type was set. After that, the book was printed on blank pages. This was called a "galley" or "proof." The proofreaders did not edit anything; their sole role was to make sure no errors were introduced into the book during the composition process. Proofreaders only made sure the book pages conformed to the edited copy and they did not make last minute editing changes. Doing that after the book was edited and typeset was considered unprofessional.

See: http://nybookeditors.com/2016/05/whats-the-difference-between-copyediting-and-proofreading/

6 See: http://www.mnn.com/your-home/organic-farming-gardening/stories/ 7-of-the-most-expensive-flowers-in-the-world.

7 Get "Morning Murmur," "Lunchtime Lounge," "Texas Teahouse" and other ambient sounds at https://coffitivity.com/. They also have Apps for Android and iOS devices.

8 Yoast offers lots of great SEO information on their site. Use their free SEO plug-in. There is no need to pay for their premium service. See: https://yoast.com/wordpress/plugins/seo/

9 This site offers 14 places to get legitimate back-links to your posts. http://www.convinceandconvert.com/digital-marketing/ build-back-links-14-easy-ways/

10 Get the Hueman WordPress template free here:

http://presscustomizr.com/hueman.

11 Statistics compiled by Felix Just, S.J., Ph.D. See: http://catholic-resources.org/Bible/NT-Statistics-Greek.htm

LEGAL NOTICES AND DISCLAIMERS

Intellectual property is cited as follows: Sources are often credited in the End Notes section.

1. Visual content without attribution is either created or copyrighted by DL Hughes, used under a paid non-attribution license or in the Public Domain.

2. In cases where a Creative Commons (CC) License element is used it is noted in the End Notes section. Various CC license versions referenced in the attribution can be viewed at https://creativecommons.org/licenses/.

3. Some material is used in accordance with Title 17 of the U.S. Copyright Act. Attribution, formal or informal, is supplied when appropriate. If you have copyright concerns, contact us via email at:

VelocityWriting@gmail.com.

4. Trademarks. All product names, logos, and brands are property of their respective owners. All company, product and service names used are for identification purposes only. Use of these names, logos, and brands does not imply endorsement.

Donald L. Hughes

DISCLAIMERS

1. This content is not intended as a substitute for professional advice. You are advised to consult a licensed professional in your geographic region for legal, accounting, medical or other professional advice so the professional can assess your particular situation.

2. The facts and opinions are offered as a general overview of the topic and your specific application of the information will vary. The author has made every effort to ensure the accuracy of the information in it was correct at time of release, but there are no representations or warranties, express or implied, about the completeness, accuracy, reliability, suitability or availability with respect to the information, products or services contained in this book for any purpose.

3. Nothing in this content should be interpreted as a promise or guarantee of earnings. Any use of this information is at your own risk. Each individual's success depends on his or her background, skills, knowledge and motivation. The use of our information, products and/or services should be based on your own due diligence, which you undertake and confirm that you have carried out to your complete satisfaction.

The author makes no warranty of any kind, either express or implied, including but not limited to implied warranties of merchantability and fitness for a particular purpose, with respect to the content or embedded links. In no event shall the author be liable for any damages (including damages for loss of business profits, business interruption, errors or omissions, whether such errors or omissions result from accident, negligence, or any other cause, or other pecuniary loss) arising out of the use of or inability to use this content, even if the author has been advised of the possibility of such damages.

4. Testimonials and examples used are exceptional results, which do not, or may not, apply to the average person, and are not intended to guarantee, promise, represent and/or assure that anyone will achieve the same or similar results.

5. Some portions of the material on this website appears in various edited or unedited forms in seminars, other website blog posts, videos, presentations, eBooks, paperback book editions, audiobooks, podcasts and online courses written, produced and copyrighted by DL Hughes and branded in varying ways.

Made in the USA
Monee, IL
25 March 2021